the 74-year-old South African Prime Minister Field Marshal Jan Smuts and Field Marshal Alanbrooke, Chief of the Imperial General Staff (CIGS). During the visit of 'our interesting but severely limited conquest' (as Churchill called it) crowds of troops mobbed him, while French civilians could only gaze incredulously as he arrived unannounced, an unmistakable figure in his Trinity House serge coat and cap, cheerfully brandishing his V-for-Victory sign and Cuban cigar.

A l.. keep
up wi.................................... d the
sea cr................................ ......Beach,
his visit to General Montgomery's headquarters, his departure from Courseulles in Rear-Admiral Vian's launch and his tour along the sectors, coded Gold, Juno and Sword, on the *Kelvin*. But for security reasons, Churchill's close inspection of the workings of his secret brainchild, the 'synthetic lagoon' forming off Arromanches – soon to be popularly known as 'Port Winston' – went unreported at the time. Now, in the words of those who travelled with him, and through film stills and photographs – many previously unpublished – we can reconstruct the events of his extraordinary day.

"Himmel! Tourists!"

Sunday Express, June 11th, 1944

Published 11 June 1944, with his cartoon captioned 'Himmel! Tourists!' Giles anticipated the first civilian visit by a day, and foresaw that millions would follow in Winston Churchill's footsteps to see the D-Day Landing beaches.

The 'Old Man' in his Element

'These are wonderful sights to see, with all these thousands of vessels.'

CHURCHILL IN A TELEGRAM TO PRESIDENT ROOSEVELT, 14 JUNE 1944

Over the weekend preceding D-Day, Churchill took it upon himself to visit General Eisenhower's personal headquarters and as many troops as he could before they finally embarked, staying overnight on his personal train nearby.

On 3 June, after a morning's work on the train (fitted with its own offices, saloon, conference room and bathroom) and lunching with Smuts and Ernie Bevin, the Home Secretary, they set out in Churchill's Rolls Royce to see the Northumbrian Division in Portsmouth and visit Southampton

> 'The train, lurking in sidings behind the south coast, had gone slightly to Churchill's head. It gave him a sense of advance headquarters and almost of directing the invasion.'
>
> FROM *CHURCHILL: A BIOGRAPHY* BY ROY JENKINS

Water to review the shipping and Mulberry Harbour elements gathered there. An eyewitness described the scene: 'The old man was in his element. He moved among the vehicles talking to everybody. The troops laughed at his sallies and some of them were not slow in answering him back. The whole atmosphere was one of expectation and tense nervous excitement. The next day he stood watching the troops embarking at Southampton. Many of them touched his coat as they passed and called for a speech. He did not want to speak, he was too full of emotion, so he called out, "Good luck, boys." A soldier called out, "Have you got a ticket, sir?" "What ticket?" asked Winston. "One like this," said the soldier, holding up a piece of paper. "It entitles me to a free trip to France." Much moved, he [Churchill] replied, "I wish I had, if only I were

ABOVE: For want of harbour anchorages, two-thirds of the 147 Phoenix caissons (204-foot long hollow concrete units with flooding valves) for the two prefabricated Mulberry Harbours were towed, assembled and 'parked' on soft mud off Selsey Bill (Sussex), the rest off Littlestone-on-Sea, near Dungeness (Kent). Unsticking them from the sea mud using Navy pumps had been one of a number of last-minute crises that had required the Prime Minister's personal intervention.

ABOVE: 5 June 1944, Lee-on-the-Solent, off the Isle of Wight, one of many settings of the largest amphibious operation in history. In the foreground is the tug anchorage ①; the large vessel to the right is the 17,500-ton depot ship HMS *Aorangi* ② and just discernible in the middle distance are Landing Ship Tanks (LSTs) ③; in the centre, HMS *Despatch* ④, the future Arromanches Port Headquarters ship. Top left are the troopships *Princess Astrid* ⑤ and the *Maid of Orleans* ⑥ – the latter sunk by a mine on 28 June. In the background ⑦ are some of the 250 road 'convoys' destined for the two Mulberry Harbours.

a few years younger, nothing could have kept me away." The tears came to his eyes. He then took a boat to Southampton Water to view the gathering armada, disappointed not to have seen as many men as he had planned.'

Harry Butcher, General Eisenhower's Chief Aide, remarked: 'Churchill had bad luck hitting the right landing places at the wrong time or vice-versa, so the PM didn't do so well. In the middle of this hide-and-seek behind the energetic motorcycle escort, the PM said to call up Ike and he'd come and see him. It was the only thing that worked OK for him, but when he arrived here his mental outlook was described by his Naval Aide, Commander Thompson, as "peevish". The PM disclosed to Ike that the King had vetoed his boat ride in the invasion. Now Winston was pouring the heat on Ike to prevent *him* from going across on D-Day, saying that Ike was too valuable, must be handy for emergency decisions, etc ... Returning to camp last night, the PM's caravan of cars and dashing motorcyclists swirled in behind unexpectedly. Filled their gas tanks and diminished our supply of Scotch,

there being some 10 or more parched mouths to moisten, and announced that De Gaulle would be sent over here to see the Supreme Commander on Sunday afternoon. "Tommy" Thompson told me we could keep him!'

On the evening of 4 June, after a stressful afternoon with an unbending General De Gaulle and amid mounting tension as the weather deteriorated sharply, Churchill returned to London. Alanbrooke found him 'in a very highly strung condition ... and over-optimistic as regards prospects of the cross-Channel operation and I tried to damp him down.'

Churchill was working, giving dictation until 3.45 the following morning. His relentless routine was legendary, his long hours and attention to detail was wearing for those much younger and closer to him. One of his secretaries, Marian Holmes, who worked through the night of 4–5 June, described him that night: 'He looked anxious but he was amiable. He has been striving for this moment for four years ... He drives himself far too hard and he nearly fell asleep over the papers.'

Operation W.C.

'Is it fair that you should then do exactly what I should have liked to do myself?'

KING GEORGE VI TO WINSTON CHURCHILL, 2 JUNE 1944

George VI with Admiral Sir Bertram Ramsay, the naval commander-in-chief of the Allied invasion, and the First Sea Lord, Admiral Sir Andrew Cunningham, as they tour Juno Beach on a 'duck' (DUKW – an amphibious tank) on 16 June.

Over lunch on 30 May Churchill had revealed to the King that he intended to join the fleet on D-Day, and the King said he would do the same. The King's Private Secretary, Sir Alan 'Tommy' Lascelles, was thoroughly alarmed: 'I shook the King by asking him whether he thought the project would be quite fair to the Queen; and whether he was prepared to face the possibility of having to advise Princess Elizabeth on the choice of her first Prime Minister, in the event of her father and Winston being sent to the bottom of the English Channel … I quickly persuaded the King without much difficulty that it would be wrong, from many points of view, for either him or Winston to carry out their projected "Overlord" jaunt.'

ABOVE: A bond of friendship and enormous mutual respect evolved between the King and the Prime Minister, despite their difference in age.

The next day Winston received a letter from the King, in his own hand, begging him not to go: a letter Churchill ignored. On 1 June the Allied Naval commander of Operation Neptune, Admiral Ramsay – who had communicated Churchill's plan codenamed 'Operation W.C.' to Eisenhower (who was 'very averse' to his going) – was invited to spell out how Churchill would sail on HMS *Belfast*. In this meeting, in the map room of the Downing Street annexe where the Mulberry model was displayed, the King suggested a cruiser might do for both of them, but 'the unfortunate man [Ramsay] … reacted violently'. Churchill then opposed the King's going – which the King accepted with good grace – while persisting in the 'Operation' against all advice. Lascelles wrote in his diary: 'Winston knows perfectly well that he oughtn't to do this, but when he gets these puckish notions, he is just like a naughty child.'

It took a second forceful letter from Buckingham Palace to get Churchill to change his mind:

ABOVE: Sir 'Tommy' Lascelles is seen here accompanying the sovereign to Normandy on 16 June, on board HMS *Arethusa*.

Friday June 2nd 1944

My dear Winston

I want to make one more appeal to you not to go to sea on D-Day. Please consider my own position. I am a younger man than you, I am a sailor, and as King I am the head of all three Services. There is nothing I would like better than to go to sea but I have agreed to stop at home; is it fair that you should then do exactly what I should have liked to do myself? You said yesterday afternoon that it would be a fine thing for the King to lead his troops into battle, as in old days; if the King cannot do this, it does not seem to me right that his Prime Minister should take his place. Then there is your own position; you will see very little, you will run a considerable risk, you will be inaccessible at a critical time when vital decisions might have to be taken, and however unobtrusive you may be, your mere presence on board is bound to be a very heavy additional responsibility to the Admiral and the Captain. As I said in my previous letter, your being there would add immeasurably to my own anxieties, and your going without consulting your colleagues in the Cabinet would put them in a very difficult position which they would justifiably resent. I ask you most earnestly to consider the whole question again and not let your personal wishes, which I very well understand, lead you to depart from your own high standard of duty to the State.

I am
Yrs v. sincerely
GRI

In his reluctant, rambling reply to his monarch Churchill concluded: 'Since Your Majesty does me the honour to be so much concerned about my personal safety on this occasion I must defer to Your Majesty's wishes, and indeed commands.'

Ramsay suggested that it might be better to wait six days beyond D-Day, when it would be safer, and Churchill would be able to go ashore. On 13 June, after his return from Normandy, the Prime Minister, and later the Cabinet, approved the idea that the King could visit the beaches and Mulberry in his turn. And so it was that the King was finally able to go – on 16 June.

Crossing on the Kelvin

'Luckily we had a perfect day, not a cloud in the sky until evening. I was on the bridge all the time and there was always something to watch ....'

12 JUNE DIARY ENTRY BY JOHN MARTIN, THE PRIME MINISTER'S PERSONAL SECRETARY

Having announced on Saturday his intention to go – and this time the King raised no objection – the next evening, on 11 June, Churchill was back on his train 'stabled at Ascot' readying himself for departure, along with a hastily convened American party of VIPs. Churchill warmly welcomed the American service chiefs, General Marshall (US Army), General 'Hap' Arnold (US Air Force) and Admiral King (US Navy), who had just flown in from Washington. After an 'admirable' dinner in the saloon (the meal featured a rehoboam of 1926 Pol Roger champagne – Churchill's favourite – and 'a grand old brandy out of balloon glasses') the Americans turned in early, leaving Churchill with Field Marshal Smuts and Bedell 'Beetle' Smith, Eisenhower's own Chief of Staff.

Past midnight they were joined by Field Marshal Alanbrooke. At 2 a.m. Churchill was still at work – wiring Eisenhower to seek assurances about the issue of gas masks to the troops.

At 7.30 a.m., after breakfast, the train quietly steamed through the low-lying morning mist into Portsmouth, arriving half an hour later. The party split, the British to the destroyer HMS *Kelvin*, the Americans to the submarine chaser USS *Thompson*.

ABOVE: Alanbrooke (right) sits by the Lewis gun as Lt Commander Robert MacFarlan RN downs his tea to the dregs. Tea was rationed from 1940 to 1952 (2oz per week in the war years) but the Royal Navy had a special allowance, consuming an estimated 4,000 tons in 1944: a vital ingredient to the British war effort both at home and abroad.

BELOW: Churchill looks astern from the bridge of the *Kelvin*, accompanied by his Naval Aide Flag Officer Lt Commander Charles Ralfe 'Tommy' Thompson (foreground, wearing glasses) and Lt Commander MacFarlan RN (second left), the commanding officer of the ship.

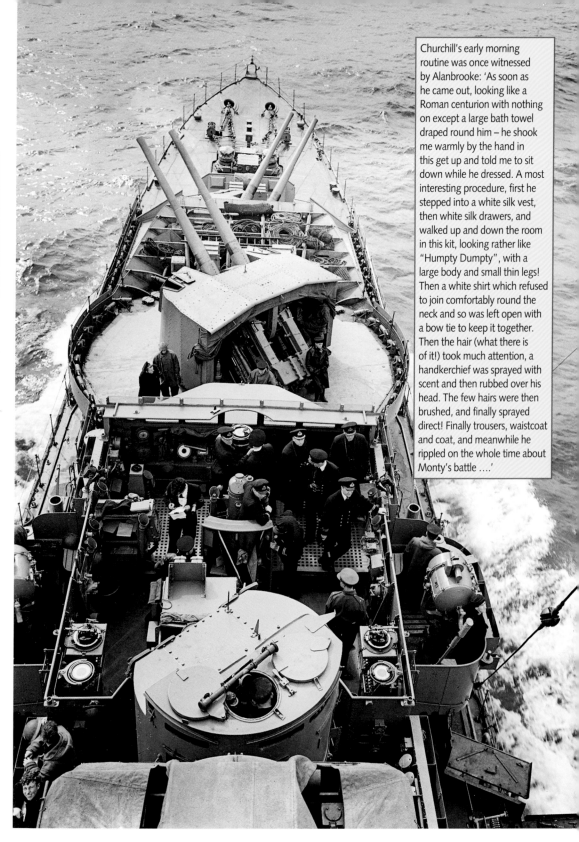

Churchill's early morning routine was once witnessed by Alanbrooke: 'As soon as he came out, looking like a Roman centurion with nothing on except a large bath towel draped round him – he shook me warmly by the hand in this get up and told me to sit down while he dressed. A most interesting procedure, first he stepped into a white silk vest, then white silk drawers, and walked up and down the room in this kit, looking rather like "Humpty Dumpty", with a large body and small thin legs! Then a white shirt which refused to join comfortably round the neck and so was left open with a bow tie to keep it together. Then the hair (what there is of it!) took much attention, a handkerchief was sprayed with scent and then rubbed over his head. The few hairs were then brushed, and finally sprayed direct! Finally trousers, waistcoat and coat, and meanwhile he rippled on the whole time about Monty's battle ....'

ABOVE: A dramatic view looking down from HMS *Kelvin*'s 'crow's-nest' onto the bridge, the 4.7-inch bow guns at the ready.

Never Such a Sight ...

'As far as the eye could see the water seemed to be covered with a stupendous mass of craft of all sizes for miles to the horizon on both sides. There can never have been such a sight in the history of the world, and I doubt if there ever will be again.'

WINSTON CHURCHILL, 12 JUNE

The entire Operation Neptune fleet stationed off the 'Far Shore' of Normandy from D-Day to the end of June was 79 per cent British and Canadian; this was to be the last major manifestation of British imperial sea-power that Churchill would ever see. Within five years much of this fleet, including the *Kelvin* itself (whose nameplate now hangs in Chartwell, Churchill's country home), had been laid up or scrapped – along with Britain's status as an imperial power.

ABOVE: Wearing sunglasses against the morning glare, Churchill takes up a sheltered position on the gunwale deck to look at the shipping.

John Martin's diary entry reads: 'The crossing was smooth but approaching the Normandy coast the sea was thickly crowded with the warships and merchant ships of the Allied navies; high above them long grey-white vapour trails were drawn across the cobalt blue sky – large formations of 'Forts' and Liberator bombers were streaming towards France, while P38 Lightnings weaved about them, glinting in the sun. It was a deeply moving sight.'

Field Marshal Alanbrooke reported on the same sight: 'We had a very comfortable journey over, and most interesting. We continually passed convoys of landing craft, minesweepers, bits of floating breakwater (Phoenix) being towed out, parts of the floating piers (whales) etc. And overhead, a continuous flow of planes going to and coming from France. About 11 a.m. we approached the French coast and the scene was beyond description. Everywhere the sea was covered with ships of all sizes and shapes, and a scene of continuous activity. We passed through rows of anchored LSTs and finally came to a "Gooseberry" [IV, off Courseulles], namely a row of ships sunk in a half crescent to form a sort of harbour and to provide protection from the sea.'

'Just after 11 a.m. we reached the beach anchorage. Off the port beam were the grey-blue lines of HMS *Nelson*, and then they passed HMS *Scylla*, flying the flag of Rear-Admiral Sir Philip Vian [Naval Commander of Eastern (British) Task Force off Sword, Juno and Gold], the ship's company lining the deck and "hip-hipping" as the *Kelvin* slipped by. Two launches closed on *Kelvin*'s starboard quarter to pick up Churchill and his party, one was Vian's blue and white barge that streaked away from the side of the *Scylla* and Admiral Vian was piped aboard the *Kelvin*. After a few hurried words Churchill, followed by Smuts and Alanbrooke, stepped into a duck and headed for the beach just west of the harbour entrance, a quarter of a mile away. The *Kelvin* edged away from shore and, passing HMS *Nelson* and HMS *Ramillies*, two of the bombardment battleships, took up a position to commence shore bombardment with her six 4.7-inch guns.'

THE TIMES, 13 JUNE 1944

ABOVE: Taken from the port deck of HMS *Kelvin*, where Churchill would have observed his escort ship HMS *Scourge* pulling past.

Field Marshal Jan Smuts (1870–1950)

The Prime Minister of South Africa was a member of the War Cabinet in both World Wars and his long and staunch friendship with Churchill went back to the First World War when he had lived for two years in Britain. In May 1944 he had been attending the Commonwealth Prime Ministers' conference and was Churchill's favoured companion for his inspection tours in England and his visit to Normandy. Smut's son, also called Jan but known as 'Jamie', who accompanied his father on all his visits, remarked: 'Between these two old friends there existed a warmth of feeling and mutual admiration that was touching to see. In public it was "Prime Minister" and "Field Marshal" but otherwise it was simply "Winston" and "Jan". In each other's company they seemed to cast the cares of the world from their shoulders and to assume a new animation. They were a tonic to each other.'

In his book *Churchill: A Biography*, Roy Jenkins gives a more blunt assessment: 'Smuts loved being at Churchill's side; he gave wise advice, vitiated only the fact that it was almost always exactly what Churchill wanted to hear ....'

ABOVE: A photographer can be seen clambering down from the *Kelvin*'s masthead ladder, one can imagine having just taken the picture on page 7.

Juno Beach

'The French population did not seem in any way pleased to see us arrive as a victorious country to liberate France. They had been quite content as they were, and we were bringing war and desolation to the country.'

FIELD MARSHAL ALANBROOKE, 12 JUNE

ABOVE: The 'duck' has come ashore and a brief discussion precedes the Prime Minister's descent onto the beach.

General Montgomery strode up in his battered old RAF Irvin jacket and, 'smiling and confident', met the party on Juno Beach. Churchill climbed down a short ladder from the 'duck'; they shook hands warmly and Montgomery showed him to the back of a jeep parked on the beach. Montgomery jumped in alongside Churchill; the rest of the party crammed into two other vehicles.

Robert Barr, the BBC Home Service war correspondent, reported a form of naval salute to Churchill's arrival on shore: 'The order was given: "three salvoes into the German lines". Mr Churchill, cigar in the corner of his mouth and his sea cap on the back of his head, smiled and raised his binoculars. And the guns of HMS *Kelvin* began to pound the German positions.'

John Martin described the short jeep trip: 'I shared one with an Admiral [Parry], three other naval officers, Smut's son [Jamie] and the driver, a very tight fit! Then we drove off through the town and into the country. The houses on the seafront [Courseulles] had been badly damaged by the bombardment but inland we were astonished by the general peaceful aspect of the countryside. Here and there buildings had been knocked about or there was a crashed plane or burnt out car, while German signs with "Minen" and skull and crossbones showed where there were minefields, possibly bogus; but generally speaking the landscape was little changed. Crops were ripening for harvest. I even saw some fat cows munching contentedly, and the people in the roads, friendly and happy, showed no marks of privation.'

Five miles inland, driving along the beautiful Seulles valley on the Bayeux road they turned off down a track, between two high stone Baroque

ABOVE: Montgomery greets Churchill as he climbs down from the 'duck' and sets foot on French soil: filmed as well as photographed, the powerful symbolism of this moment was minutely documented for posterity.

'Soldiers busy unloading landing craft stood in amazement at the sight of the familiar Trinity House cap, the cigar, and the two fingers raised in a V-sign. Men not actively engaged in unloading rushed up to the duck: some stood to attention and saluted; others held back, waved and clapped their hands. General Smuts, smiling cheerfully, was at work with his cine camera as the party clambered into the waiting jeeps and drove off.'
THE TIMES, 13 JUNE 1944

ABOVE: Churchill lights up his eponymous La Corona cigar as he sets off for Creullet in the jeep with Montgomery. In 1945 he wrote to their donor, Samuel Kaplan, a New York Jewish businessman: 'those wonderful cigars have cheered my long path through war'.

pillars and plunged into a small wood on a hillside behind the château of Creullet. Where the track emerged into the sunshine onto the flat lawns of the château grounds, they seemed to have stumbled into a rural idyll. They had arrived at the Tac HQ. The stunning view across the Seulles valley to one of William the Conqueror's castles on a rocky outcrop is likely to have appealed to Churchill's sense of history: in 1356 the castle had been captured by the English. General Montgomery, in buoyant mood, pointed the way to his map caravan, an articulated lorry designed by Monty himself as his operational command centre, and parked on the edge of the wood.

The Luncheon Party

'We are surrounded by fat cattle lying in luscious pastures with their paws crossed!'

CHURCHILL TO ALANBROOKE AT CREULLET, 12 JUNE

ABOVE: Churchill with Alanbrooke and Montgomery; the only known colour photograph of Churchill taken on 12 June 1944.

At Tac HQ, Churchill was delighted to be so near the front line and later remarked: 'There was very little firing or activity. The weather was brilliant. We drove through our limited but fertile domain in Normandy. It was pleasant to see the prosperity of the countryside. The fields were full of lovely red and white cows basking or parading in the sunshine. The inhabitants seemed quite buoyant and well-nourished and waved enthusiastically. Montgomery's headquarters, about five miles inland, was in a château with lawns and lakes around it. We lunched in a tent looking towards the enemy. The General was in the highest spirits. I asked him how far away was the actual front. He said about three miles. I asked him if he had a continuous line. He said "No".'

The three caravans behind the château were shrouded in camouflage netting and webs of signalling wire. On the open lawn a Union Jack flapped limply on a small portable flagpole.

The château's owners, an elderly retired colonel and his wife, Monsieur and Madame de Druval, were required to keep their shutters overlooking the caravans closed. Following bombing the previous night they were clearing out their glass and chinaware and responded to a request from Montgomery, through an embarrassed aide-de-camp, for what he termed a '*vase de nuit*'. Unsure as to what was required, they provided a vase decorated with pink flowers – but the battlefield commander was lacking a chamber pot, not a flower vase!

Churchill – having shown his pass to the sentry – was first taken into the brand-new bespoke map caravan backed into the trees. The caravans alongside had been captured from the Italians in North Africa and had since served Montgomery's austere personal needs. Famously, Montgomery asserted: 'I would turn out of this caravan only

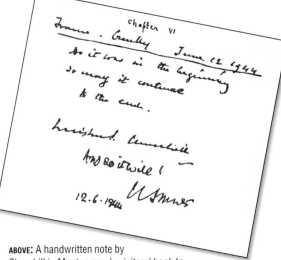

ABOVE: A handwritten note by Churchill in Montgomery's visitors' book to which Smuts confidently added his own comment: 'And so it will!'

for two people: the King and Winston Churchill.' One had formerly been used by Rommel, whose photograph hung on the wall. Today Montgomery's caravans are on display in the Imperial War Museum collection at Duxford (Cambridgeshire).

Montgomery delivered a 30-minute explanation to Alanbrooke, Churchill and Smuts. Churchill emerged reassured and relieved by the General's impregnable confidence, gratified and surprised that the countryside appeared so prosperous, and delighted that everything, as he was told, was 'going to plan'. The terrible reality of Caen, whose burning glow was still lighting the night-time sky from Creullet, the shared fate of so many French towns and villages, and the sufferings being inflicted upon the French elsewhere, was beyond his eye.

Churchill was then invited to settle to a simple lunch in the open, marked by the constant, if sporadic, 'crump' of larger naval artillery in the background. Montgomery's mess waiter produced some genuine Camembert cheeses – not seen in England since 1940.

John Martin and the others drifted off. In his diary Martin reported: 'The PM went with the CIGS [and Smuts] had a conference with Monty at his HQ. Meanwhile with the rest of the party I hurried through some sandwiches and then went for a stroll in the nearby village [Creully]. It is full of military patrols, but some of the inhabitants were going about or looking out of their windows. German placards were still on the walls (full of *Verboten*) and there was one amusing one of the PM shown as a hideous cigar-smoking octopus, with tentacles over half of Europe.'

ABOVE: The château of Creullet photographed shortly after noon on 12 June 2008. In 1944 the caravans were concealed behind the château on the edge of the woods to the right. The stone gatepost on the left also features in the view across the Seulles valley towards Creully castle (page 15).

Tac HQ: Personal Impressions

'The French civilians do not look in the least depressed; there is plenty of food, plenty of vegetables, cows, milk, cheeses and very good crops. The people appear well fed, and the children have good boots and clothing.'

MONTGOMERY IN A NOTE TO PHYLLIS REYNOLDS, HIS SON'S GUARDIAN

Sergeant Norman Kirby, responsible for security within the grounds of the château at Creullet, had carefully vetted Churchill and his other guests' papers (only the King would pass unchecked). There were few guards and no barbed wire around this nerve centre of the battle. Yet snipers were still active and, as Montgomery had warned Churchill, they included women – eight had been shot dead in the vicinity.

The previous day there had been an alarming breach of security within 50 yards of where the

Winston and Monty

A number of exchanges between Churchill and Montgomery have become legendary. For example, when Churchill suggested that Monty study logistics, Montgomery doubted that the Prime Minister should become involved in such technical matters. 'After all,' he said, 'they say that familiarity breeds contempt.' 'I would like to remind you,' Churchill rejoined, 'that without a degree of familiarity we could not breed anything.'

ABOVE: After emerging from the conference the group's attention is caught by what appears to be a 'Hun' air raid. Alanbrooke has put on his glasses to peer up at it; the bearded figure in the middle is Premier Smuts of South Africa; the man on the left is Lt General Sir Richard O'Connor, commander of VIII Corps, who had escaped from an Italian POW camp the previous year. Montgomery observed of the air battle, 'Everyone was rather alarmed. Winston was rather pleased.'

The Château de Creully, where a week after Churchill's visit the BBC set up a studio in the square tower and radio correspondents of many nations broadcast the daily 'War Report' to the world. A small BBC museum here may now be visited in season. This photograph was taken at lunchtime on 12 June 2008, 64 years to the day after Churchill was here.

conference was taking place. Kirby recalls: 'At 4 a.m. on June 11th I was woken up by a guard to interrogate a German soldier who had been caught *inside the camp perimeter* and only a few yards from General Montgomery's caravan. So much for security. He was aged 18, a Sudeten German in the infantry. He said he was alone, but in the shock and confusion of the D-Day invasion his comrades had left him behind. No-one had been giving him food and owing to a shortage of rations he had given himself up. He had been hiding in a hole in the rhododendron bushes by the château for three days and was very scared and hungry. As this frightened adolescent with trembling fingers emptied his pockets of his few possessions, including a photo of his mother, we were given a quite different view of the German army from the one publicised by our news media. After being offered food and the inevitable mug of tea – which he regarded with distrust until I drank from it – our prisoner was kept under guard until daylight and then taken to a POW cage. From then on no thicket, shrubbery or spinney within our camp boundary escaped the closest scrutiny ....'

Winston and Alanbrooke

On 7 May 1944 Alanbrooke wrote in his diary: 'He [Churchill] was an astounding mixture, could drive you to complete desperation and to the brink of despair for weeks on end, and then would ask you to spend a couple of hours or so alone with him and would produce the most homely and attractive personality. All that unrelenting tension was temporarily relaxed, he ceased to work himself into one fury or another, and you left him with the feeling that you would do anything within your power to help him carry the stupendous burden he had shouldered.'

In return, Churchill said of Alanbrooke: 'When I thump the table and push my face towards him what does he do? Thumps the table harder and glares back at me.'

ABOVE: Montgomery explains the battle to King George VI inside his map caravan. Churchill would have had a similar 'Monty Special' (as they were sometimes termed), described by Alanbrooke as 'all as usual wonderfully clear and concise'.

Courseulles-sur-Mer

'Had the PM, CIGS and Smuts here today; all in very good form; the PM very obedient and I pushed him away at 15.00 hours and would not let him go beyond my HQ.'

MONTGOMERY TO MAJOR GENERAL FREDDIE DE GUINGAND, 12 JUNE

Churchill left Normandy at around 4 p.m. from the east quay of the little harbour of Courseulles after a brisk walkabout. Official sources speak of a '7-hour tour ashore among the troops' but Montgomery's letter to his son's guardian, Phyllis Reynolds, and Alanbrooke's diary ('We then returned to Courseulles having watched a raid by Hun bombers') make it clear that despite appearances, and Churchill's evident enjoyment of risk-taking, too many dangers lurked in the countryside to allow him to stray from the security corridor created for him between the port and Tac HQ. Churchill was, in fact, sent straight back to Courseulles after only three hours ashore.

'On reading this I see I have scarcely mentioned the troops of whom we saw a great many. They looked fit and in very good heart and gave the PM a great welcome when they recognised him and there was some difficulty in clearing a way to the launch.'

JOHN MARTIN'S DIARY ENTRY, 12 JUNE

ABOVE: Churchill's reception at Courseulles by Canadians, mostly dock workers and men of the No.2 Port Repair and Construction Group. In the foreground, his hands behind his back, is Lt Commander MacFarlan of the *Kelvin*; to his immediate left, Flag Officer Lt Commander 'Tommy' Thompson, the Naval Aide who travelled with Churchill throughout the war. Carrying binoculars, Rear-Admiral W.E. Parry, Admiral Sir Bertram Ramsay's chief of staff, will accompany the Prime Minister to the Mulberry Harbour and serve as his guide, while MacFarlan is to return directly to his ship, now anchored there. In immaculate civvies, wearing a broad-brimmed hat (and also visible on the opposite page) is John Martin, Churchill's Principal Private Secretary. Behind the Prime Minister Montgomery's famous badged beret marks him out in the crowd, while Field Marshal Alanbrooke makes his way between the jeeps. Note also the cameraman standing above the crowd to capture Churchill boarding Rear-Admiral Vian's launch to leave Normandy.

COURSEULLES-sur-MER
L'Écluse du Bassin - La Pêche à la Sardine

ABOVE: The sleepy inner harbour before the war. Boys on bikes gather by the lock gates where locals fish for sardines. The Corbel sawmill with its industrial chimney stack and unloading gantry has long since disappeared, but formed the backdrop of Churchill's progress along the east quay to the awaiting launch, which on 12 June 1944 was tied fore and aft to the two bollards seen either side of the motor car. The houses on the left still stand today.

The 'missing' hours are explained by Churchill's visit to what was still one of the greatest secrets of the war – the 'synthetic harbour' (as Churchill described it) being created in front of Arromanches. The Prime Minister's own version of events deliberately omits any reference to the Mulberry Harbour: 'We made a considerable inspection of our limited bridgehead. I was particularly interested to see the local ports of Port-en-Bessin, Courseulles and Ouistreham. We had not counted much on these little harbours in any of the plans we had made for the great descent. They proved a most valuable acquisition, and soon were discharging about two thousand tons a day. I dwelt on these agreeable facts with which I was already familiar, as we drove or walked around our interesting but severely restricted conquest.'

ABOVE: This still from a film made of the visit conveys the excitement of the crowd and the intensity of the conversation taking place between Montgomery and Churchill as they stride along the east quay together.

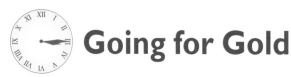

'Troops rushed his car and surrounded it until it could not move. Some wanted to shake hands, others to give the Prime Minister a pat on the back.'

THE TIMES, 13 JUNE 1944

ABOVE: A crowd of troops and dockers has formed along the opposite, western quay of the inner (locked) harbour and onto a barge. Note the white ambulance landing craft (left). The VIP party (Rear-Admiral Parry, Alanbrooke, Churchill, Flag Officer Thompson and Rear-Admiral 'Bill' Tennant) is ready to go, but someone is missing – the South African Premier Field Marshal Smuts, who seems to have got separated from the group in the dense crowds of men. However, Montgomery is anxious to hand his visitors over to the Navy and get back to Tac HQ and to the business in hand, directing the battle.

That night Montgomery dashed off a cheery note to Phyllis Reynolds: 'As it is I am being bombarded with visitors – all very nice for them, but it does take up a great deal of time. I am well installed in my caravans in the very pleasant Normandy country; and I am delighted to be leading the open life again. I can wear again my battle clothes, corduroy trousers and grey sweater; PM in good form and for once he was prepared to admit that I was in charge: he was quite prepared to take orders and do what he was told – which was a great change!!'

ABOVE: With Field Marshal Smuts back on board, Churchill raises his cap to the 'huzzahs' echoing out from both quays of the little port as the party leaves the inner harbour behind and heads out for the sea. The famous Trinity House cap is preserved at Chartwell.

Churchill left Courseulles and its modest but efficient 'Gooseberry' breakwater behind and headed west towards the next line of sunken ships, off Arromanches, 7 miles away. At Le Hamel the launch was taken up to Gold Beach, within hailing distance, so Winston could see troops and tanks disembarking from beached landing craft. Here the Prime Minister was able to call out to the men, and time on his stopwatch the emptying of its cargo of tanks of a grounded LCT. At this time all the bustle and activity of on-shore logistics was on the beaches, not at Arromanches itself: by 12 June a total of 190,674 men, 51,319 tons of material and 27,836 vehicles had been landed in the British sectors while at Mulberry B, which was still forming, just 1,500 tons of stores had come ashore. Indeed by 17 July only 2,145 men of 573,579 in the British sector had been landed at Mulberry B, and none of the 130,793 vehicles landed across British beaches. It was only on his second visit, between 20–23 July, that Churchill was able to see the full potential of the harbour, handling stores, vehicles and men together.

ABOVE: Before Gold beach, Rear-Admiral Tennant points to the west where a demonstration of the different working parts of the prefabricated harbour, and of naval firepower, was waiting.

Here We Go Round the Mulberry

'We then went to the new harbour being prepared west of Hamel. There we saw some of the large Phoenixes being sunk in place and working admirably. Also "bombardons" to damp down waves, "Whales" representing wonderful floating piers, all growing up fast.'

ALANBROOKE'S DIARY ENTRY, 12 JUNE

The party – shadowed by an escort ship laden with visitors, engineers, naval and military personnel – passed Le Hamel, at the end of Gold Beach, and a shuttling convoy of 'ducks' heading up the newly cut road to the top of the cliffs at St-Côme. Alongside, an incomplete LST roadway connected to a Bailey bridge (a portable prefabricated truss bridge) on land jutted out to sea; it was destined for tanks, soldiers and hospital ships. Two other roadways, and the beginnings of a fourth, were emerging out of the village creek itself, a mile further west.

The floating roadway convoys of which the roads were composed, although ingenious in conception and effective once in place, were by far the most complex of all the harbour elements and were experiencing many problems of seaworthiness. Shipment and assembly had been made an Army responsibility, commanded onshore by Brigadier

A.E.M. 'Wally' Walter RE CBE. The first had set out at 3.30 p.m. from Lee-on-the-Solent on 8 June (see page 3) but by 12 June five convoys – and a number of men – had already been lost. Others were being forced to turn back. Under the stress of being towed broadside on, in the heaving, twisting, yawing and rolling action of the roads, the brittle concrete floats were splitting, their concrete bollards were being torn out by the roots, and the erection tanks were coming adrift.

On 13 June Rear-Admiral William G. Tennant CB, responsible for the movement and assembly of the Mulberry/PLUTO project (and who would also accompany the King three days later), ordered all convoys to come in spans of three, not six, and only in daylight. This created a backlog that led to the release of 28 convoys (totalling 2½ miles in length) – together with the daily quota of four Phoenixes

---

Mulberry B on 12 June: a convoy section makes its approach. Churchill's launch passed from east to west (right to left) along the line of 15 sunken merchant ships (known as 'Corncobs', they made up 'Gooseberry III'), past the forming roadways, past his own ship HMS *Kelvin*, waiting in the lee of HMS *Alynbank* after its gunnery salute off Juno Beach, and past HMS *Despatch*, the harbour's newly-arrived headquarters ship. Note the 'mini-spuds' (steel legs) on the bridging, needed to keep pressure off the floats at low tide. To overcome the anchorage problem for the emerging roadways, 400-yard long anchor cables were stretched out over the sands by means of special floating shuttles. At the end of each cable were uniquely designed 'kite' anchors that bound the roadways into the seabed: under tension the anchors behaved in a balance of forces similar to the uplift of an inverted kite and became entirely buried by the pull of the cables. The floats nearest to the shore were bolted to the sea wall.

The present D-Day Landings Museum is situated onshore between the two roadways; the anti-tank wall (left) borders its car park.

Phoenix caissons — Western stores pier roadway — HMS *Despatch* — HMS *Kelvin* — Kite anchor cables — Corn

In this view looking towards Arromanches, Beckett (see panel right) can be seen standing on the end of the eastern stores pier roadway.

and four pierheads – in response to an excellent weather forecast. The 480-foot long roadway convoys crossed calm waters overnight and all arrived and were within sight of the harbour at daybreak on 19 June. But none made it – and nearly a month would elapse before any more would attempt the Channel crossing. In the end about 40 per cent of the tows would be lost, most in the famous storm of 19–21 June.

'The pier was braced up like a woman's corset!' Here Allan Beckett MBE (1914–2005), the bridge designer to whom this quote is attributed, personally supervises the alignment of the bridge ends on their 'erection' (flotation) tanks, which would be discarded once the bridge was in position. He now has his own memorial, inaugurated on 6 June 2009, next to the D-Day Museum in Arromanches. The memorial displays his portrait with a copy of a kite anchor and, alongside, a bridge section.

Bridge convoy

Eastern stores pier roadway

Corncobs

'Winnie' the Whale

'They must float up and down with the tide. The anchor problem must be mastered .... Don't argue the matter. The difficulties will argue for themselves.'

WINSTON CHURCHILL TO LORD MOUNTBATTEN, IN A MEMO
THAT LAUNCHED THE MULBERRY PROJECT, 30 MAY 1942

The most crucial and ingenious part of Port Winston was the sliding pontoon which allowed unloading in all tidal conditions. Its original genius was Bruce (later Sir Bruce) White KBE (1885–1983), the brilliant civil engineer promoted to Brigadier and in 1941 put in charge of a War Office department known as Transportation 5 (Tn5). He himself responded to Churchill's famous memo (above) by adapting the working principles of a 1923 dredger that stood on 'spuds'. The first pierhead to undergo trials at Cairn Head was launched on 8 April 1943 and christened 'Winnie' by her Clydeside builders. At the time of launching this 1,000-ton platform was the largest all-welded water-borne structure built in Scotland. The prototype took four months to construct – but the remainder had to be manufactured in just four weeks each. The first production pierhead was launched on 26 January 1944.

The delays in manufacturing pierheads and roadways worried Churchill; as the author of

Code Name Mulberry, Guy Hartcup, observed: 'The conception of the floating pier was never absent for long from the Prime Minister's mind and, in fact, the development of Mulberry continued to hold his attention until the end of the war. He even kept a working model of the scheme next to the War Room in Whitehall. Early in March he was already fretting that the "matter is being much neglected. Six months [have elapsed] since I urged the construction of several miles of pier".'

On 11 June the first pontoon set out from the straits of the Isle of Wight: 'Winnie' was by then one of 22 pierheads, and No.588 was destined to inaugurate the stores pier at Arromanches for Churchill's visit. Unfortunately, with the roadway delays, the platform had to wait until 14 June before being connected up so Vian's launch was unable to use it. However, the platform's technical capacities were captured on film (see below): towed into position, its 89-foot high steel legs, 'spudded up' to maximum height and swaying slightly, were lowered

ABOVE: On 12 June pierhead 588, with its 89-foot high 'spuds', was captured on film before the cliffs of Tracy-sur-Mer, which can also be seen in the background of the top right picture.

On board the 4,850-ton converted cruiser HMS *Despatch* was the Joint Command shared by Captain C.H. Petrie DSO RN, the Naval Officer in Command (NOIC) of the Port Construction Force, and Brigadier 'Wally' Walter, the Army Officer commanding. The latter had already disembarked from the converted paddle steamer HMS *Aristocrat* on D-Day at Le Hamel (Gold Beach) and was running his side of operations (road construction, demolition, etc) from Arromanches itself. This photograph was taken on the morning of 12 June, looking down from Caisson 65 towards HMS *Despatch*, where the ship lay berthed stern to HMS *Alynbank*, and now permanently sheltered by the Phoenix line.

at the rate of a yard a minute until becoming embedded on the sandy bottom on its pointed feet. It had no need of anchors as its own legs served the purpose. The photograph (left) shows the difference in the height of the spuds; a single diesel-electric winch motor lifted the platform six inches out of the free-floating position to steady it. Churchill's famous stipulations of 1942 had been worked out, the solutions found and every Whale pierhead destined for the Mulberries arrived safely and served their purpose.

Demonstrating its ability to fix itself in deep water, pierhead 588 lowered its 'spuds' to the seabed almost a mile from shore. Each spud pierhead had 19 men on board. The cliffs of Saint-Côme, east of the village, appear behind.

Phoenix Planting

'You couldn't see daylight between one caisson and the next.'

CAPTAIN HAROLD HICKLING

'The shock we should have suffered if it had been known that the casual choice of the word "Mulberry", used as a "cover-plan", was actually mentioned in the Bible in Luke xvii, 6, where it says: "And the Lord said, If ye had faith as a grain of mustard seed, ye might say unto this Mulberry tree, be thou plucked up by the root, and be thou planted in the sea; it should obey you."'

LT COLONEL VASSAL C. STEER-WEBSTER RE (HEAD OF THE WAR OFFICE BRANCH COORDINATING THE PROJECT) TO COLONEL JOHN EISENHOWER, SON OF THE SUPREME COMMANDER, GENERAL DWIGHT D. EISENHOWER

Turning back towards the breakwater, Churchill would have observed a perfectly aligned row of six 6,000-ton concrete caissons, the 'extension arm' of the Gooseberry breakwater, but with its western end blocked off by a mis-planted caisson. Unfortunately, no sooner had Rear-Admiral Vian signalled on 10 June that 'all had been done to the great satisfaction of all' than the following night unit 18 collided with its tug, cracking the Phoenix open. The unit swiftly filled and settled askew and athwart the western end of the Phoenix breakwater. It stopped further development to the west and created an awkward wreck at what was destined to become the northern entrance, where two more units had been planned.

Attention therefore turned to the creation of the next breakwater, 700 yards further west: the 'Detached Mole'. However, on 11 June, in strong currents and a patch of rough weather, the tugs found it impossible to restrain the first lone unit 36; it drifted as it filled and sank, also settling out of position. An additional difficulty was that once the concrete ledge that characterized each caisson was under the sea, it would take on a list and the tugs no longer had anything to push against. Planting was therefore suspended while the Naval Officer in Charge (NOIC) reviewed the situation for the next day when HMS *Despatch* was due to berth.

On 12 June the normal daily influx of four Phoenixes resumed. It was decided to plant two units each end of unit 36 – but restoring the correct alignment, not butted up against it (see map on back cover). This process was greatly helped by using unit 36 as an anchor, and Churchill would have witnessed part of this operation.

Unit 60

Line of six Phoenix caisson with Bofors guns

'The Phoenix looked like a block of flats being towed by a taxi … It was no easy matter to hold these unwieldy rectangular concrete ships in a tideway with a cross-wind on their high sides, during the 22 minutes which, with all flooding valves open, they took to sink ….Yet with skilful handling of tugs and cool judgement, our "Planter" [Lt Commander A.M.D. Lampden RN] placed them not to an accuracy of feet but of inches ….'

CAPTAIN HAROLD HICKLING

HMS *Despatch* (above) – fitted with anti-aircraft guns, communication equipment and a telephone landline – took up its new role on 11 June. On 12 June the ship anchored in its definitive position just 200 feet from the Phoenix breakwater, thereby creating an additional shelter for landing craft. The ship is berthed almost stern to the slewed Corncob HMS *Alynbank* (marked by its crane and anchor; see map on back cover). At 2.07 p.m. on 7 June the *Alynbank* was the first ship to be sunk and, for similar reasons to unit 36, had settled out of line).

Churchill visited Captain Petrie on HMS *Despatch* after the bombardment demonstration, transferring via a gangway to HMS *Kelvin* which had come alongside, to rejoin Rear-Admiral Vian and Lt Commander MacFarlan, amid ecstatic scenes from sailors packed on the decks to see the Prime Minister off.

Photographed on 12 June close to unit 18 and looking east. HMS *Despatch* has not yet arrived. Later in the day the ship anchored in the lee of the Phoenix line (above) in readiness for Churchill's arrival on board. HMS *Despatch* would remain there throughout the life of the harbour as the Port HQ.

nit 42

Crane on stern of
HMS *Alynbank*

Corncobs
line

LEFT: Photographed from unit 42 on 12 June; the wrecked unit 18 is clearly visible beyond unit 60, while the 'A1' type Phoenix under tow (the largest, travelling at four knots) is destined for the 'Detached Mole'. The 'tids' (Tug Invasion Deployment) manoeuvre to take over from the large ocean tug; each Phoenix had to be kept under way until it reached its predetermined planting position.

A Parting 'Plug at the Hun'

'Since we are so near, why shouldn't we have a plug at them ourselves before we go home?'

CHURCHILL TO REAR-ADMIRAL VIAN

ABOVE: Churchill heads out for the mile-long 'bombardon', 200-foot long hollow bolted steel cruciform rafts now in place; each of the 24 rafts was steadied by 2,000 tons of seawater inside, plus 22 anchors and chains.

Before returning to ship, Churchill's launch sped out the short distance beyond the 'Detached Mole' to observe the mile-long steel boom made up of 200-foot long steel cruciform rafts known as 'bombardons' (of which there were 24), and to witness a dramatic series of salvoes from the monitor HMS *Roberts*.

Alanbrooke observed, 'Winston said he had never been on one of His Majesty's ships engaging the enemy and insisted on going aboard. Luckily we could not climb up owing to seaweed on the bilges as it would have been a very risky entertainment had we succeeded.'

After Churchill's aborted attempt to board the monitor the party turned back to sheltered waters. Once back on board HMS *Kelvin* it was clear that Churchill was not content to remain a spectator, for as BBC war correspondent Robert Barr reported: 'In the afternoon we toured the whole of the British beachhead from Arromanches to Ouistreham, sailing inshore and very slowly, Mr Churchill inspecting the shore all the way along with his binoculars and as we reached Ouistreham we continued to sail past the end of the British beachhead, and the buzz went round that we

were about to fire on the enemy. Our crews were alerted, guns were loaded and we still sailed slowly along past the beachhead, past the coastline of enemy territory and then it happened – something that caused a furore in the House of Commons next morning, for Mr Churchill leaned over from the bridge and shouted "Fire!". The guns fired on some unknown target and fired again and again and the *Kelvin* turned smartly to port and raced away from the German beaches.'

Churchill himself said of the event: 'We were of course well within the range of their artillery, and the moment we had fired Vian made the destroyer turn about and depart at the highest speed. We were soon out of danger and passed through the cruiser and battleship lines. This is the only time I have ever been on board one of His Majesty's ships when she fired "in anger" – if it can be so called. I admired the Admiral's sporting spirit. Smuts too was delighted. I slept soundly on the four-hour voyage to Portsmouth. Altogether it had been a most interesting and enjoyable day.'

The 'interesting and enjoyable' – and very long – day was concluded in their respective diary entries by both John Martin and Field Marshal Alanbrooke:

Looking like a flat-iron, HMS *Roberts* was a stable gun platform with a shallow draft to allow it to fire close inshore. In this film still it prepares to fire from its pair of 54-foot long 100-ton gun barrels (formerly part of the armament of First World War battleship HMS *Resolution* and fitted in early 1944). It took 490lbs of cordite to fire the 1,938lb 15-inch shell over its range of 18 miles. In the foreground is the launch with Churchill, Smuts and Alanbrooke on board. This still is taken from a film that may have been shot from the high conning tower of HMS *Despatch*, but it is careful not to reveal any reference to the Mulberry, although the cliffs of Tracy-sur-Mer (west of Arromanches) locate the shot with precision. One of the two 15-inch guns mounted on HMS *Roberts* dominates the entrance to the Imperial War Museum today.

'We were not back to England till ten at night, after one of the most memorable days I have ever spent. It was a thrilling time and everyone was immensely impressed ….'; 'We got on board the PM's train where we found General Marshall and Admiral King. We dined on the way back to London where we arrived shortly after 1 a.m. dog tired and very sleepy!'

Close inshore and east of the British Landing Beaches area, on Churchill's orders HMS *Kelvin* fires parting shots (discreetly set to safe) at the occupied shoreline over the cliffs east of Cabourg. Note the escort boats in these pictures and those on page 28.

A Jolly Day?

'I had a jolly day on Monday on the beaches and inland … how I wish you were here!'

<small>TELEGRAM FROM WINSTON CHURCHILL TO PRESIDENT ROOSEVELT AFTER HIS RETURN TO ENGLAND, 14 JUNE</small>

Of his on-board dinner during the evening of 12 June, Churchill, sunburned and contented, remarked, 'We dined together in a happy mood. They [General Marshall and Admiral King, the US Army and Navy Chiefs] were highly pleased with all they had seen on the American beaches and full of confidence in the execution of our long cherished design.'

On his return to London a note was passed to him in his famous map room: three waves of 'robot bombs', the V1s, were on their way across the Channel. Germany's response to Overlord and Mulberry had been to launch its own secret weapon: a new type of war was about to begin.

That same day …

- Generals Eisenhower, Marshall, Arnold and Admiral King landed at Le Ruquet, Omaha Beach, to be met by General Bradley for a visit of Omaha and Utah.

- At 6.48 a.m., Aunay-sur-Odon (Calvados) was levelled by RAF bombers and 145 civilians killed.

- The Americans took Carentan (Manche), creating a single beachhead from Utah to Sword.

- Regulars of the German army, the Wehrmacht, returned to Oradour-sur-Glane (Limousin) to unsuccessfully conceal the scattered calcinated remains of 642 villagers shot and burned alive in the church and village barns two days earlier by the SS Das Reich. They left at midday.

- The SS Das Reich departed from Tulle (Limousin) leaving 99 'partisans', hanged three days before, dangling from the lampposts in the village square. It would take 11 more days for the Das Reich to reach Normandy, delayed by actions of the resistance and Allied bombing, and leaving 4,000 civilian victims in their wake.

- This day's chilling 'allocation' from the suburb of Diosgyor (Hungary) transported 8,647 Jews in three trainloads to Auschwitz.

- In Poland, Reichsminister Alfred Rosenberg ordered the 'Hay Action', the kidnapping of 40,000 children aged 10–14 for slave labour, 'in order to enfeeble the biological potential of the Slav race'.

- Facing 228 German divisions in the east, Stalin had heralded his vast Operation 'Bagration' against German occupied areas – planned for 21 June – by attacking Finland.

- Twenty-seven V1 flying bombs were launched towards Greater London: the first such attack.

In the evening sun, HMS *Kelvin* sails past Royal Navy bombardment ships in line of battle. By the end of the month Operation Neptune was over.

HMS *Kelvin* seen from HMS *Scourge*, surrounded by ships of Vian's Eastern Task Force.

RIGHT: Churchill's 'jolly day' telegram.